tibet

MARION ELLIOT

GLOBAL • CRAFTS

tibet

GLOBAL DESIGNS FOR NEW LOOK INTERIORS

David & Charles Trafalgar Square Publishing

For Duncan and Katrina Goodwin

A DAVID & CHARLES BOOK

First published in 2000
Text copyright © Marion Elliot 2000
Photography and layout copyright © David & Charles 2000
Printed and bound in France by Pollina - n°80885

First published in the UK in 2000 by David & Charles
Brunel House, Newton Abbot, Devon

ISBN 0 7153 1089 5

First published in the United States of America in 2000 by
Trafalgar Square Publishing
North Pomfret, Vermont 05053, USA
ISBN 1-57076-172-8

A catalogue record for this book is available from the British Library.

Commissioning editor   Lindsay Porter
Art editor   Ali Myer
Assistant editor   Jennifer Proverbs
Text editor   Sarah Widdicombe
Designers   Chris and Jane Lanaway
Special photography   Stewart Grant
Styling   Lisa Brown

Contents

tibet
Introduction

> *Tibet, the mystic land of the Grand Lama, joint God and King of many millions, is still the most impenetrable country in the world.*

Tibetan Buddhism
L Austin Waddell

For centuries, Westerners have been drawn to the romantic image of the ancient kingdom of Tibet. This mysterious land, ringed by mighty mountain ranges, covers a vast landscape so far above sea level that it is called the 'Roof of the World'.

Protected from outside influence by the inaccessible peaks of the Himalayas, the Tibetans lived in near isolation for many centuries, communicating only with their neighbours, China and India. What developed was a unique civilization powered by an innate, unpretentious genius for design. That is what makes this fascinating country such a wonderful source of

Beaten metal has been used to create a distinctive mirror frame.

A window blind was inspired by multi-coloured prayer flags.

inspiration for the home designer. Mysterious and ornate monasteries on isolated mountain passes, the elaborate head-dresses worn by rural women and the abstract graphic designs created by strikingly modern-looking Tibetan architecture are just three examples of the diversity of design sources waiting to be tapped.

The Tibetan people have suffered much in the past 50 years and many aspects of their way of life have been all but destroyed. But happily, international concern for the country and the high profile of its spiritual leader, His Holiness the Dalai Lama, have drawn attention to Tibet,

revealing its culture to us in all its glory.

Photographs abound of the multi-coloured robes

of the Buddhist monks, the wandering lifestyle of

the nomads and the brightly decorated interiors

of Tibetan houses, all

of which offer a rich

source of inspiration.

Tibet is a land of

texture and contrast.

The broken, patchy

texture of a monastery

wall sets off the smooth,

Fake fur and felted wool evoke the cosy Tibetan chuba.

golden surface of its roof; the soft, shaggy edges

of a sheepskin tunic accentuate the roughness of

a hand-woven shirt. Use these ready-made

contrasts to kick-start your ideas; for example, the

fur-edged bed throw on page 46 was inspired by

the double texture of the traditional sheepskin coat, the *chuba*. Add a bold splash of rich, warm colour to a simply furnished room, using only one or two well-chosen objects as focal points. Draw inspiration from the flashes of brilliant colour covering the walls of the great monasteries and create an atmosphere of contemplative serenity with incense and flickering candlelight.

Take advantage of the current trend for natural, organic materials like felt and wool and use the woollen blankets that cover the tents of nomad families as your influence. It would be a simple job to create a private area in a corner of a room or garden with plain woollen throws or blankets giving cover and shade, or shelter from a breeze. The same idea could be adapted to make a canvas or linen canopy above a bed, or a clever screen to hide an unattractive view.

Metal leaf is used to cover a papier mâché bowl.

" *Then, in the distance, I see golden domes shining in the barren hills: the Potala, with its miracle of smooth rounded shapes rising in the blue sky, glowing like a vision.* "

Touching Tibet
Niema Ash

9

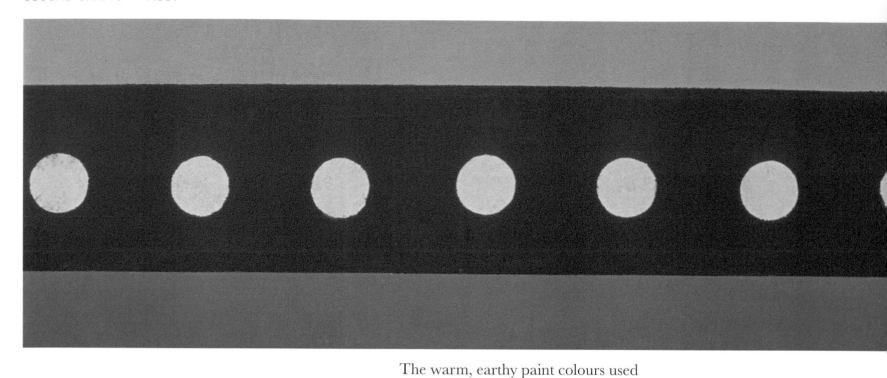

> "*Tibet has symbolized for many the archetypal holy land that we all seek.*"

Tibetan Voices
Brian Harris

The warm, earthy paint colours used for the walls of secular and religious Tibetan buildings alike can be used to dramatic effect in the home. They might be too strong in large doses, but a thin band of plain colour above a large area of rich, earthy red or yellow ochre can look extremely sophisticated. The dotted band shown in the bathroom paint scheme on page 68 demonstrates this: it could not be simpler, but nevertheless adds a graphic focus to the room, bringing warmth to an area that could feel very cold and clinical.

Warm earth tones typical of Tibetan secular architecture can be used to striking effect in the home.

The Tibetans have an obvious love of strong colour, but show great taste and a well-developed design sense when applying it to their buildings. Many monasteries and homes are painted with bright bands of colour, but these are set against a pure white background and are not overpowering. This is a good pointer when using strong colour: a little goes a long way and controlled splashes of colour work better than large, solid areas, which tend to make rooms look small. One way to introduce colour is to confine it to accessories like the satin ribbon cushion in the living room scheme on page 36. The bright, saturated colours make a dynamic splash against the neutral paint scheme, lifting the atmosphere of the room without looking garish.

The simple and unpretentious Buddhist philosophy, which encourages compassion and

"Tibet is a country of devastating beauty and great harshness, a dual nature reflected in the Tibetan character, which is both fierce and gentle."

The World of the Dalai Lama
Gill Farrer-Halls

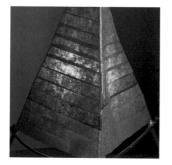

An unusal twig lamp base with paper shade combines natural textures.

humility, appeals strongly to many of us today who are disillusioned with the hectic pace and growing commercialism of life. Many people have turned towards spiritually uplifting practices such as yoga and meditation in an effort to counteract the stresses of their day-to-day existence. Address this yearning for peace and serenity by using carefully chosen colour schemes and natural fabrics in your home. After all, what could be more soothing than to sit awhile in a simple, uncluttered room, painted in earthy colours like the great monasteries of Tibet?

All the photographs in this book have been chosen for their inspirational qualities. Each contains unusual and exciting elements that can be combined in any number of ways to fit into your room scheme. Notice small details, such as contrasting stitching on lengths of cloth, the

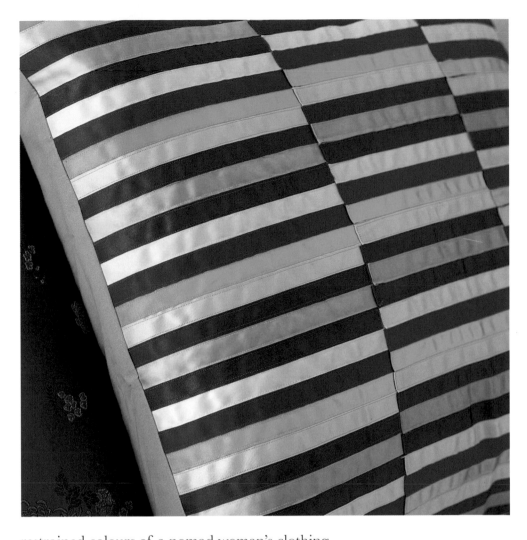

Tibetan aprons influenced the design of this cushion cover.

restrained colours of a nomad woman's clothing,

the power of the same colour repeated many

times in a group of monks' robes, and the

contrast between leather and wood in a Tibetan

skin boat. These starting points should spark off

all sorts of ideas for making striking and

harmonious accessories that will bring a sense of

calm and order to your home.

tibet
The Kitchen

15

Hand-woven Carpets

Tibet is famous for its beautiful, richly decorative, hand-knotted carpets. Probably the best-known examples are the mysterious tiger rugs, based on tiger skins but often abstracted into a pattern of stripes. Other stylized patterns, such as these flowers, are also prevalent. Carpet-making is an important source of income for Tibetan refugees in Nepal and India.

This table runner is made from finely woven, hopsack linen and is decorated with a repeating motif of ornate flowerheads. The evenly spaced flowers are painted in bright, jewel colours that stand out strongly against the cool green background. A thin band of fuchsia-coloured satin ribbon is sewn at the top and bottom of the runner to frame the flowerheads.

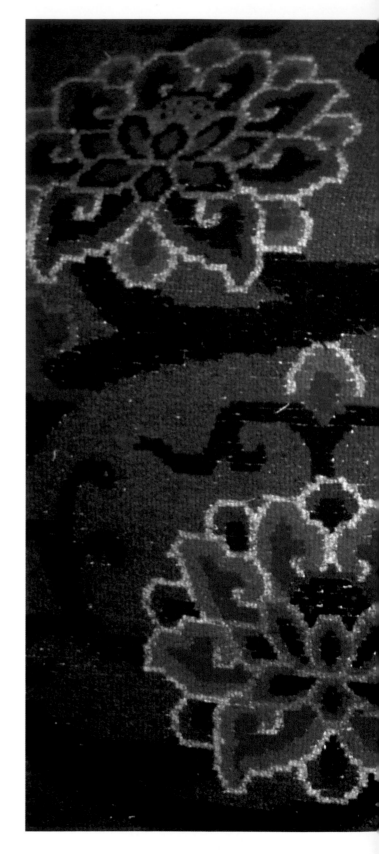

Flower Table Runner

Materials & Equipment

- Green hopsack linen
- Tape measure
- Scissors
- Ruler
- Dressmaker's pins
- Tracing paper and pencil
- Carbon paper
- Newspaper or plastic sheet
- Iron-fixable, water-based fabric paints
- Old saucer
- Thin, pointed artist's paintbrush
- Cotton pressing cloth and iron
- 1m (1¼yd) fuchsia satin ribbon, 8mm (⅜in) wide
- Sewing machine and threads to match fabrics

1 Cut a piece of hopsack linen 43cm (17in) wide by your desired runner length. Press the fabric in half lengthwise to mark the centre line. To find the position of the flowers, measure a point 25cm (10in) above and below the centre line and mark with pins. Continue measuring outwards to the ends of the runner, pinning every 50cm (20in) along it. Each pin indicates the centre of a flower motif.

2 Trace the flower pattern from the back of the book. Place the tracing centrally over a pin, on top of a sheet of carbon paper. Re-draw over the lines to transfer the motif. Repeat to transfer as many flowers as you need.

3 Cover your work surface with newspaper or a plastic sheet. Using slightly dilute fabric paint in a dark colour and a thin, pointed paintbrush, outline all the flowers and leave to dry.

4 Fill in the flowers with fabric paint, softening the colours with a little white fabric paint if desired. Leave the runner to dry.

5 Place the runner face down on clean cotton fabric and, following the paint manufacturer's instructions, iron the backs of the motifs to fix the colours.

6 Press under a 1.5cm (⅝in) hem all the way around the runner. Tuck under the raw edges, pin the hems and machine stitch in place. If your fabric has an attractive selvedge at each end of the runner, this can be left unhemmed.

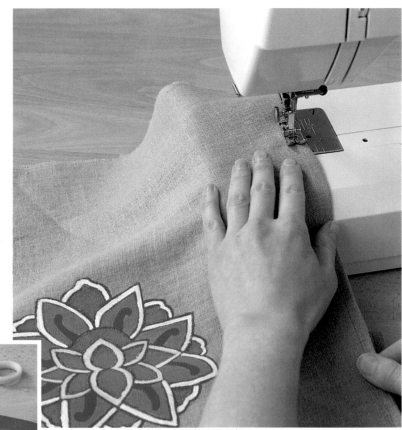

8 Machine stitch the ribbon in place, sewing as close to either side as possible. Press the wrong side of the runner thoroughly before using it.

7 Cut two lengths of satin ribbon, each 40cm (16in) long plus 3cm (1¼in). Pin a piece of ribbon at either end of the runner, just above the hemline, turning under the raw ends of the ribbon.

Butter Lamps

Altars in Tibetan monasteries are places of intense colour and light. During worship, richly coloured religious images and statues draped in white ceremonial scarves, called *khatas,* are bathed in the flickering light of brass and silver butter lamps. The hand-beaten metal lamps contain a wick suspended in yak butter, which burns like candle wax, illuminating the faces of the deities. In Buddhism, fire symbolizes wisdom, and destroys ignorance.

These miniature glass lanterns are recycled glass jars, just wide enough to contain a tea light. A simple handle has been made from fine-gauge galvanized wire, looped into a thin collar around the necks of the jars. The glass is frosted to give a soft, warm glow. The lanterns can be arranged in rows, or clustered together to make a dramatic concentration of light.

Frosted Glass Lanterns

Materials & Equipment

- 1mm ($^1/_{32}$in) gauge galvanized wire
- Wire cutters
- Clean glass jars
- Pliers
- Dowel or broom handle
- Protective face mask
- Frosting varnish
- Tea lights

SAFETY NOTE: Do not leave the lanterns to burn unattended.

1 Cut a piece of wire long enough to fit around the neck of a jar, plus 20cm (8in). Grip the wire with the pliers, 5cm (2in) in from one end, and twist it gently round to make a small loop.

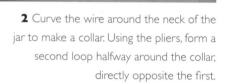

3 Hold the collar in position. Using the pliers, twist the free ends of the wire tightly together to keep it in place. Trim the ends and press them back against the neck of the jar.

2 Curve the wire around the neck of the jar to make a collar. Using the pliers, form a second loop halfway around the collar, directly opposite the first.

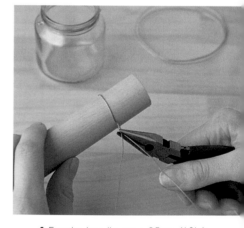

4 For the handle, cut a 25cm (10in) length of wire. Find the centre and wrap it around a piece of dowel or a broom handle. Cross over the wires, and twist them tightly together several times, directly below the dowel, to make a loop. Slide the loop off the dowel.

5 Trim the ends of the wire to 10cm (4in) long. Pass the ends through the loops in the collar at the neck of the jar.

6 Grip one end of the wire with the pliers and curl it up to make a small, open loop. Repeat to curl the other end. Hook the open loops through the loops in the collar. Close them tightly, making sure that the wires are the same length and the lantern hangs level.

" The room is glittering with light

from butter lamps arranged in rows on

a low bench before a shrine. "

Touching Tibet
Niema Ash

7 Wearing a face mask, and working outdoors if possible, spray each jar with frosting varnish. Place a tea light, in its metal holder, inside each glass lantern.

23

Hand Gestures

I n Tibetan Buddhism, there is an extensive language of hand gestures, called *mudra*, which convey the attributes of deities. These are used in ceremonies and are shown in paintings and sculptures. The hand of Lord Buddha, for example, signifies protection. Palm upwards, it represents unlimited giving. When the right hand is extended, with the palm downwards towards the earth, it signifies the enlightenment of the Buddha.

In this painted frieze, a pair of clasped hands, indicating greeting, are flanked by flowerheads. The panel is roughly plastered and rubbed back to make a textured surface, which absorbs the paint unevenly, giving it an aged appearance. The motifs are filled in with vibrant colours, embellished with metal leaf, and the plaster is sealed with clear wax polish, softening the outlines of the paint.

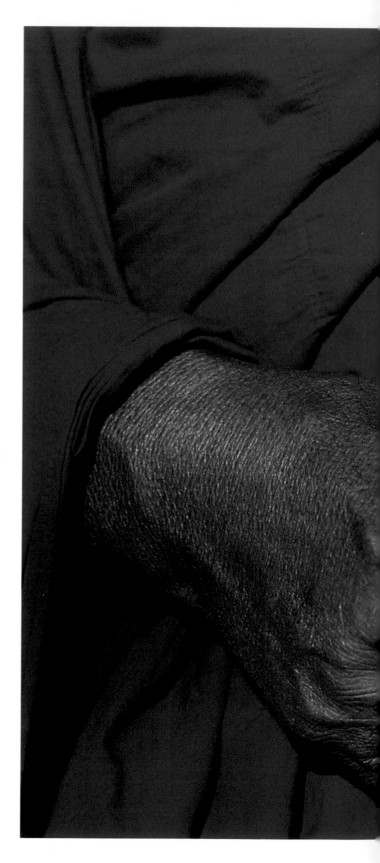

Gilded Plaster Frieze

Materials & Equipment

- PVA adhesive (all-purpose white glue)
- Paintbrushes, including thin, pointed artist's paintbrush
- Panel of 12mm (½in) plywood, 105 x 30cm (41 x 12in)
- Water-based acrylic wood primer
- Craft knife
- Protective face mask
- Old plastic mixing bowl
- Powdered surface filler (spackle)
- Rubber-edged spreader
- Medium- and fine-grade sandpaper
- Large paintbrush
- Pencil and long metal ruler
- Gouache paints in vivid green, dark pink, white, blue, orange and yellow
- Old saucer • Tracing paper
- Carbon paper
- Water-based gold size • Dutch metal leaf
- Soft, wide brush • Clear wax polish
- Soft cloth • 2 mirror plates and screws
- Screwdriver

1 Apply a coat of dilute PVA adhesive (white glue) to both sides of the plywood to seal the surface. When dry, prime the front with one coat of acrylic wood primer. Using a craft knife, key the primed surface in a cross-hatched pattern.

2 Wearing a face mask, mix a bowl of surface filler (spackle) following the manufacturer's instructions. Spread a thin, slightly rough layer of filler over the front of the board, using a rubber-edged spreader. Leave the board to dry overnight in a warm place.

3 Wearing a face mask and working outdoors if possible, lightly sand back the dry filler. Keep sanding until the surface is generally smooth, but interesting pits and marks remain. Brush away the remaining dust with a wide, dry paintbrush.

4 Using a long metal ruler, draw a 5cm (2in) border around the edge of the board.

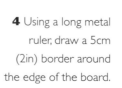

5 Using gouache paints, paint the background vivid green. Paint the border dark, chalky pink. Apply a second, lighter shade of pink (made by mixing dark pink and white) to the border to intensify the colour. Apply two more coats of green paint, in a slightly lighter tone, to the background. Use a dry paintbrush to give the colour a broken, patchy appearance.

6 Draw a faint pencil line along the centre of the board. Trace the flower and hands motifs from the back of the book. Place a sheet of carbon paper centrally over the pencil line. Position the tracing of the hands on top and redraw over the lines to transfer the image. Repeat to transfer two flowers to either side of the hands.

7 Using a thin, pointed paintbrush, outline the hands and flowers in watery, dark pink paint. Keep the lines thin, and not too pronounced.

8 Mix some fairly thick, light pink paint. Fill in the hands, painting directly over the green background to give a patchy effect. Paint the bracelet light blue. Fill in the flowers with orange, yellow and pink paint. Apply several layers to build up a deep, rich colour.

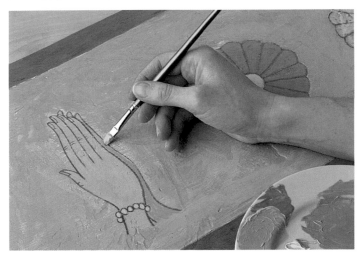

9 Once the paint is dry, apply a thin coat of gold size to the centre of each flower. When the size is tacky, gently rub on a patch of metal leaf, using a soft, wide brush. Leave to dry overnight.

10 Using fine-grade sandpaper, rub the centre of each flower very gently to remove a little of the metal leaf and give a patchy effect. Apply a coat of clear wax polish to the picture, avoiding the metal leaf, with a soft cloth to seal the surface. Buff the polish to give a soft sheen. Screw a mirror plate at either side of the frieze.

tibet
The Living Room

"*The second and third floors are used as living rooms and are equipped with fireplaces or iron stoves, in which wood or cow dung is burned, for cooking or making tea.*"

The Wonders of Tibet
Chen Heyi

Painted Walls

The Tibetan people have a wonderfully rich sense of design. Their homes are simply but vividly decorated, with walls painted in a variety of styles. They may be painted to dado (chair rail) height in one strong colour, then topped off with simple horizontal bands in contrasting colours. More elaborate schemes contain painted decorations. On the exterior of buildings, too, bands of contrasting paint emphasize the elegance of Tibetan architecture.

Contrasting felt bands have been used to border this boldly coloured floorcloth. The cloth is divided into two and appliquéd with an embroidered plant motif and a row of flowerheads. Felt is traditionally made from yak wool in Tibet, and is used by nomads to make the walls of their large tents. It is a very durable material and will make a hardwearing floorcloth.

Banded Floorcloth

1 Cut a piece of blue felt measuring 150 × 105cm (60 × 41in) and a piece of purple felt measuring 105cm × 53cm (41 × 21in). Trace the plant and flower motifs from the back of the book and enlarge as required on a photocopier. Trace the motifs, including the flower centres, onto the plain side of the fusible paper.

Materials & Equipment

- 1.5m (1¾yd) blue felt, 120cm (48in) wide
- 0.6m (¾yd) purple felt, 120cm (48in) wide
- Tape measure
- Scissors
- Tracing paper and pencil
- Iron-on fusible paper
- Felt in dark yellow, white, dark red and light yellow
- Pressing cloth and iron
- Dark green embroidery silk and needle
- Dressmaker's pins
- Piece of hessian (burlap), to fit back of floorcloth
- Rubber-based adhesive
- 5.5m (6yd) woven hessian (burlap) webbing
- Sewing machine and threads to match fabrics

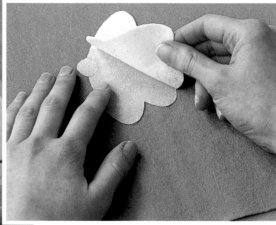

2 Place the paper, glued side down, onto appropriately coloured felt and iron over the back to fuse it to the fabric. Cut out the motifs.

3 Press under 3cm (1¼in) down one long edge of the purple felt. Peel the backing paper from the plant and flowers. Place the plant, glue side down, in the centre of the fabric. Cover with a damp pressing cloth and iron to bond it to the felt. Bond the centres to the flowers, then bond the flowers onto the felt in the same way.

4 Position the large white flowers at the left-hand side of the blue fabric, facing inwards. Bond them to the felt, then bond the flower centres on top.

5 Using a soft pencil, lightly draw veins onto the leaves. Embroider the veins in dark green embroidery silk, using small backstitches.

6 Pin the purple felt onto the blue, matching all edges. Machine stitch the two pieces of felt together.

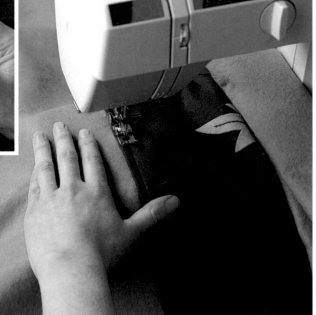

7 Cut strips of red felt 11cm (4¼in) wide to fit around all four edges of the floorcloth. Cut strips of dark yellow felt 5cm (2in) wide to fit down the short sides. Press all the strips in half lengthwise.

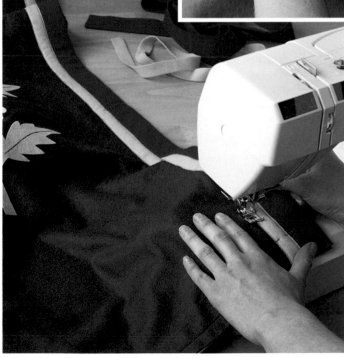

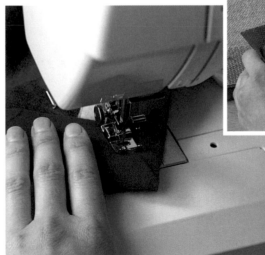

8 Pin red felt strips to the sides of the floorcloth, enclosing the raw edges. Machine stitch in place. Pin the dark yellow strips next to the red and machine stitch these in place, too.

9 Position red felt strips along the top and bottom of the floorcloth, folding under the corners to mitre them, and pin in place. Machine stitch as before.

10 Cut a piece of hessian (burlap) the same size as the finished floorcloth. Press under a 15mm (½ in) hem all round and glue the hessian to the back of the floorcloth using rubber-based adhesive. Glue hessian (burlap) webbing around the outside of the hessian to neaten the edges.

Women's Aprons

In Tibet, a common feature of traditional women's dress is a long apron, called a *bandigan*. The aprons are formed from three narrow strips of finely striped, hand-woven fabric and vary in colour: some are woven from earthy, natural-hued threads, while others are dazzlingly bright. The aprons are assembled with the pattern of stripes in the central panel raised above those in the outer panels. This gives a vibrant, almost three-dimensional appearance.

The dazzling stripes of this ribbon cushion are formed by stitching short lengths of narrow satin ribbon onto a plain backing. The ribbons are arranged in thin panels, imitating the design of the aprons. The cushion is backed with medium-weight, sky-blue cotton and closes with a simple envelope flap. Buttons, press-studs (snaps) or ribbon ties can be added if desired.

Striped Ribbon Cushion

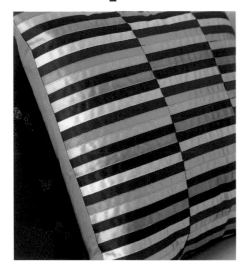

Materials & Equipment

- 70cm (28in) medium-weight, pre-shrunk white cotton fabric, 120cm (48in) wide
- Scissors
- Satin ribbon, 10mm (³⁄₈in) wide, in a variety of colours
- Pencil and long ruler
- Fabric adhesive
- Dressmaker's pins
- 70cm (28in) medium-weight, pre-shrunk sky-blue cotton fabric, 90cm (36in) wide
- Sewing machine and threads to match ribbon colours

1 For the cushion fronts, cut two 58cm (23in) squares of white cotton fabric. Cut 22cm (8½in) strips of ribbon in a variety of colours.

> *When I washed my Tibetan apron,*
>
> *I never let it hang down…but always held it*
>
> *face up as I flapped the water out.*

Tibetan Voices
Brian Harris

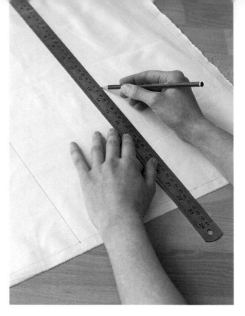

2 Using a pencil and ruler, draw a 15mm (½in) seam allowance all the way around one cushion front. Divide the remaining area into three equal panels.

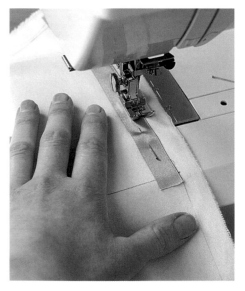

3 Dot a very small amount of fabric adhesive onto the back of the first piece of ribbon. Position the ribbon onto the cushion front, inside the first of the three panels. Line up the ribbon with the pencil line at the top of the fabric and overlap the seam allowance at the outside edge. Use matching thread to machine stitch the ribbon in place.

4 To attach the second piece of ribbon, dot adhesive onto the back as before. Tuck under one raw edge and position the ribbon on the fabric inside the second panel, to overlap the raw end of the first piece of ribbon. Stitch in place with matching thread as before. Repeat with the third piece of ribbon, gluing and stitching it into place in the third panel.

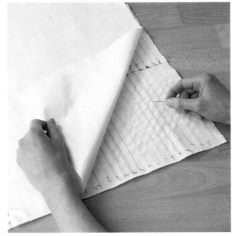

5 Continue gluing and stitching the ribbons to the cushion front, alternating colours to make a repeating pattern. When all the ribbon is in place, pin the second cushion front to the back of the first, matching corners and edges exactly. Machine stitch in place.

6 Cut two rectangles of sky-blue cotton, each measuring 58 x 45cm (23 x 18in). Press under a 15mm (½in) hem down one long side of each piece. Tuck under the raw edges, and stitch the hems in place.

8 Clip the corners of the cushion cover and trim the seams slightly. Turn the cushion through and shake out. Use a pin to pull out the tips of the corners into points.

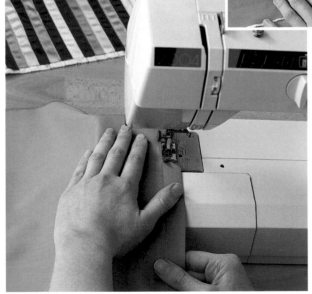

7 Pin one back to the front of the cushion, right sides together, with the hemmed edge to the centre. Pin the second back in place, with the hemmed edges overlapping, to make a flap closing. Machine stitch the backs to the front using a 15mm (½in) seam allowance.

Prayer Wheels

Prayer wheels are hollow cylinders of metal, inscribed with mantras. They are filled with tightly rolled pieces of paper bearing printed prayers. The prayer wheels may be small enough to hold in the hand, or over a yard tall and mounted in rows, but they all revolve, and with each revolution the prayers contained inside are deemed to have been recited.

This papier mâché bowl is richly gilded in imitation of the beautiful brass prayer wheels found all over Tibet. The bowl is first painted with a coat of rich, deep red paint, which will glow warmly through the wafer-thin metal leaf. Dutch metal leaf is then applied over the entire bowl, so that the surface takes on the appearance of polished brass. Where natural breaks occur in the metal leaf, the deep red paint shows through, producing a subtly distressed finish.

Gilded Bowl

Materials & Equipment

- Large plastic bowl, to use as a mould
  - Petroleum jelly
    - Newspaper
- Children's PVA adhesive (all-purpose white glue)
  - Plastic bowl • Palette knife
    - Scissors
      - Protective face mask
- Medium- and fine-grade sandpaper
  - White emulsion (latex) paint
    - Dark red acrylic paint
    - Old saucer • Paintbrush
    - Water-based gold size
      - Varnishing brush
      - Dutch metal leaf
      - Soft, wide brush
      - Shellac varnish
- Sand • Incense sticks

1 Smear the inside of the mould with a thin layer of petroleum jelly so that the papier mâché can be removed easily. Coat the rim and the top 2cm (¾in) of the outside of the mould as well.

2 Fold several sheets of newspaper together. Grip the top right-hand corner of the paper and pull it sharply down to tear long, even strips, each about 2.5cm (1in) wide. Tear a big pile of strips before you begin making the papier mâché.

3 In a plastic bowl, dilute the PVA adhesive (white glue) with water to the consistency of single cream. Dip a strip of newspaper into the glue, wipe off the excess with your fingers and lay it into the mould, overlapping the rim. Add more newspaper, overlapping the strips slightly and pressing out any air bubbles as you work. Add about eight layers of paper, then leave the mould in a warm place for 48 hours to dry.

4 Once the papier mâché feels dry, carefully insert a palette knife between the paper and the mould. Working your way around the mould, lever out the paper shell and leave it upside down to dry thoroughly.

5 Trim away the excess paper from the rim of the papier mâché bowl. The rim of the mould will have left a slight impression in the papier mâché, and this will make a good cutting guide.

6 Tear small, thin strips of newspaper about 1cm (⅜in) wide. Coat each piece with diluted adhesive and stick to the rim of the bowl, overlapping the cut edge and sealing it neatly.

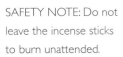

7 Wearing a face mask, lightly sand the bowl smooth. Prime the papier mâché with a coat of white emulsion paint, then paint the bowl dark red and leave to dry.

SAFETY NOTE: Do not leave the incense sticks to burn unattended.

8 Using a varnishing brush, paint a thin, even coat of gold size over the surface of the bowl. Leave the size to dry until it is tacky but not wet.

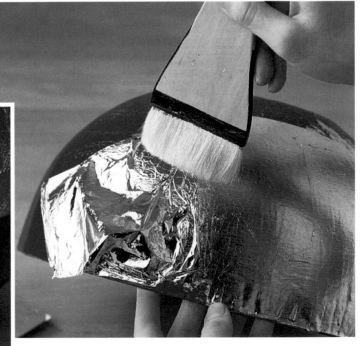

9 Slowly slide sheets of metal leaf onto the sticky size. Pat each one gently down with a soft, wide brush. Cover the entire bowl, overlapping the sheets slightly. Leave to dry for about three hours, then rub over the leaf with the soft brush to remove any excess flakes. Seal with a coat of shellac varnish. Fill with sand and add incense sticks.

tibet
The Bedroom

❝ The great bell goes and awakens everyone hitherto slumbering, and it is soon followed by the great conch-shell trumpet-call… ❞

Tibetan Buddhism
L Austin Waddell

43

Tibetan *Chuba*

S heep and yaks are an essential part of Tibetan life. Yaks provide milk to make tea, cheese and butter. The latter is also used to fill lamps and to make sculptures. Yak wool is used to make thick, felted cloth for blankets, while thick sheep hides are used for the traditional Tibetan coat known as the *chuba*. This is a knee- or ankle-length garment, sometimes with extremely long sleeves, that wraps around the body and is tied at the waist. It is worn woolly side in and has a distinctive, shaggy edge.

This bed throw is made from thick, brown, felted wool fabric. It is trimmed with shaggy fake fur in imitation of sheep hide. Lengths of pale brown and orange ribbon are stitched over the raw edge of the fur trim to neaten it. Small, beaded cloth motifs in a stylized flower design are attached in a row along the upper edge.

Felted Bed Throw

Materials & Equipment

- 2m (2¼yd) brown blanket-weight woollen fabric, 150cm (60in) wide
- Dressmaker's pins
- 7m (8yd) shaggy fake fur trim
- Scissors
- Tacking (basting) thread and needle
- Wide-toothed comb
- 7m (8yd) burnt-orange grosgrain ribbon, 15mm (½in) wide
- Iron
- Beaded decorations (or woven fabric, if the throw will be cleaned frequently)
- Ruler
- Fabric adhesive
- 7m (8yd) sage-green cotton tape, 10mm (⅜in) wide
- Sewing machine and threads to match fabrics

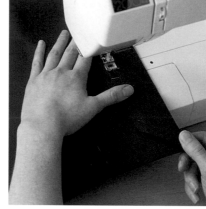

1 Press under and pin 5cm (2in) hems all round the piece of thick brown woollen fabric, mitring the corners as you go. Machine stitch the hems in place.

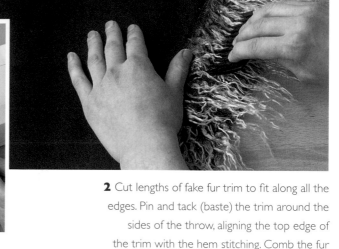

2 Cut lengths of fake fur trim to fit along all the edges. Pin and tack (baste) the trim around the sides of the throw, aligning the top edge of the trim with the hem stitching. Comb the fur straight to prevent it from catching in the sewing machine needle.

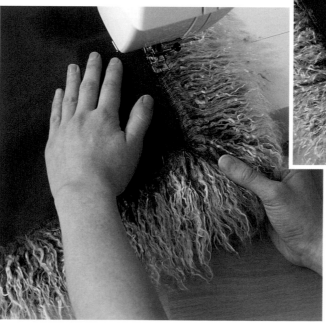

3 Machine stitch the trim to the throw, using a long stitch and sewing close to the upper edge. If necessary, comb the fur fibres flat as you sew. Remove the tacking (basting) stitches.

4 Cut lengths of orange ribbon to fit around the sides of the throw, plus 15mm (½in) at either end. To attach the first piece, turn under the excess to hide the raw end, and pin in place.

5 Turn under the raw end on the second piece of ribbon. Pin it to the throw at right angles to the first piece, covering the end to neaten the corners. Repeat to attach the remaining lengths, then machine stitch in place.

6 Pin and machine stitch the tape to the throw, directly above the orange ribbon. Sew the strips on one at a time, overlapping the corners as before.

7 Press the reverse of the throw, avoiding the fur trim. Space the decorations evenly along the top edge of the throw and mark their place with pins. Glue them in position with fabric adhesive and leave to dry.

" Early next morning I awake to a winter wonderland and remember we are over 14,000 feet high. "

Touching Tibet
Niema Ash

Prayer Flags

Brightly coloured prayer flags are a common sight in Tibet, fluttering in the breeze above houses and from poles along mountain passes and pilgrim ways. Printed by hand using wooden blocks, the cloth flags bear mantras and blessings. It is believed that these are carried to the heavens as the flags move in the breeze. The five colours used – yellow, green, blue, red and white – symbolize the elements.

For the bedroom window blind, fabric squares, imitative of the flags, have been made into pockets and stitched to a fine cotton to produce a display facility for contemplative objects. The pockets are decorated with a hand-painted mantra, *om mani padme hum*, the prayer of the Bodhisattva Avalokiteshvara, the Supreme Lord of Compassion and the patron deity of Tibet.

Pocket Window Blind

Materials & Equipment

- Red and saffron yellow cotton sari fabric
- Scissors
- Iron
- Dressmaker's pins
- Sari-style embroidered trim (optional)
- Paper
- Needle and thread
- Masking tape
- Photocopies of Tibetan Buddhist mantra, in different sizes (see templates at the back of the book)
- Fine artist's brush
- Black, iron-fixable, water-based fabric paint
- Bamboo
- Sewing machine and threads to match fabrics

1 Cut out a piece of red fabric the same width as your window, plus 6cm (2⅓in) on all sides for hems. Turn in 3cm (1¼in) of fabric along each side and press, then fold over a further 3cm (1¼in) to encase the raw edges and press again. Pin the hems and machine stitch in place.

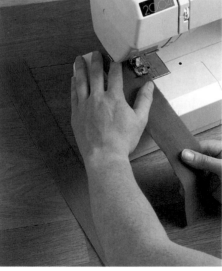

2 To make the ties, cut seven strips of saffron cotton, each 40 × 10cm (15¾ × 4in). Press in half lengthwise and machine stitch each one along the side and top edges. Clip the corners of the ties, then turn through and press flat. Finally, turn in the raw edge at the bottom of each tie and slipstitch.

3 With the right side of the fabric facing up, lay the ties at equal intervals along the top edge, with the centre of each tie lying a little below the fabric edge. Pin the centre of each tie to the fabric, then machine stitch each one in place, reinforcing with a second row of stitching. Press up the lower half of the ties. (At this stage, an embroidered trim to resemble a sari border could be sewn to the top and bottom edges of the blind.)

4 To make a pattern for the pockets, cut a paper square measuring 18 × 18cm (7 × 7in) and pin the pattern to a double thickness of saffron yellow fabric. Cut around it and repeat as many times as is necessary to provide the required number of flag pockets for the size of your blind.

5 Using masking tape, attach each pocket to a photocopied motif. Don't worry if you can't fit the whole of the text onto the squares – it adds to the abstract appearance of the blind. Next, using a fine artist's brush, 'trace' the characters onto the pockets with fabric paint. When dry, fix the paint by ironing the fabric on the reverse side, following the paint manufacturer's instructions.

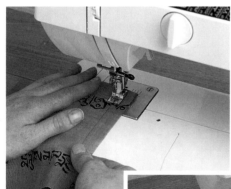

6 Press the top 2cm (¾in) of each pocket to the right side of the fabric to make a flap and machine stitch both sides of the flap 1cm (⅜in) in from the edge.

7 Clip the corners, then turn through the pockets. Use a pin to pull out the corners of the flap. Turn in and press 1cm (⅜in) of fabric all the way round each pocket. Machine stitch the flap in place on each pocket front.

8 Spread the blind on a flat surface, and with the right side facing up, pin the pockets in position, spacing them evenly and starting approximately 15cm (6in) from the top edge.

9 Machine stitch the pockets in place. Press flat, then tie the blind to a length of bamboo. Fill the pockets with lightweight items.

Yak-skin Boats

Tibetan yak-skin boats, called *cowas*, are very light, so that they can be carried easily on land by the boatmen. The framework is made from thick branches, firmly lashed together. This is then covered in yak hides, sewn together to make a strong, lightweight patchwork. The boats are powered by wooden oars arranged in pairs along the sides.

The paper covering of this twig lampshade is inspired by the tightly stretched hulls of Tibetan skin boats. Three twigs are lashed together to form a tripod, the legs being kept in place with shorter lengths of twig. The resulting framework is covered with narrow bands of handmade paper, stretched tightly between the twigs. The shade is placed over a low-wattage light bulb that shines softly through the paper.

Twig and Paper Lampshade

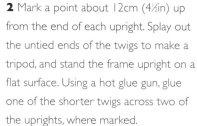

1 Using a hacksaw, cut three 70cm (28in) lengths and three 50cm (20in) lengths of thin twig. Bunch together the three longer twigs and tie them tightly at one end with thin brown string, 6cm (2½in) down from the top.

Materials & Equipment

- Hacksaw
- Thin twigs
- Thin brown string
- Pencil and ruler
- Hot glue gun
- Scissors
- Fire retardant
- Light and dark brown handmade paper
- Craft knife and cutting mat
- Safety ruler
- PVA adhesive (all-purpose white glue)
- Small glass bottle
- White gravel
- Bottle light fitting
- Decorative 25-watt bulb

2 Mark a point about 12cm (4½in) up from the end of each upright. Splay out the untied ends of the twigs to make a tripod, and stand the frame upright on a flat surface. Using a hot glue gun, glue one of the shorter twigs across two of the uprights, where marked.

3 Glue the remaining two twigs to the uprights to complete the lampshade frame, making a wigwam-type structure.

SAFETY NOTE: Do not leave the lamp switched on when unattended.

4 Cut three 60cm (24in) lengths of thin brown string. Securely tie the end of one piece at each intersection, and bind it tightly, wrapping the string around diagonally in both directions. Tie off the ends and trim.

5 Following the manufacturer's instructions, apply fire retardant to the light and dark brown paper. Cut several 3cm (1¼in) wide strips of light brown paper and three 3cm (1¼in) wide strips of dark brown paper.

6 Starting from the intersections at the base of the frame, glue strips of light brown paper across one side, from twig to twig. Overlap each strip slightly, and trim the ends to follow the angle of the uprights as you work. Stick on three light brown strips, then one dark. Complete the shade with light brown paper. Repeat to cover the remaining two sides of the frame, stopping about 15cm (6in) from the intersection at the top of the frame.

7 Fill a small bottle with enough white gravel to weight it. Insert a 25-watt bulb into the light fitting. Place the fitting into the neck of the bottle, making sure it fits snugly.

8 Place the lampshade centrally over the bulb, ensuring there is a clearance of at least 15cm (6in) all round between the shade and the bulb.

tibet
The Bathroom

> *"Bhuddist: Ablutions at*
>
> *the initiation of a monk*
>
> *represent the washing away of*
>
> *the past as a layman."*

An Illustrated Encyclopedia of
Traditional Symbols
J C Cooper

Ceremonial Head-dresses

In Tibet, the tiered arch appears in many forms, including in traditional ceremonial head-dresses and in the amulets that Tibetans wear around their necks. These amulets are delicately wrought from metal and contain a picture of a spiritual figure, often His Holiness the Dalai Lama.

This metal mirror frame is made from fine-gauge aluminium foil, attached to a wooden base. The metal is cut to size, then hammered gently on the reverse with a rounded, ball-head hammer, to indent the surface. This leaves a pitted, raised surface on the other side of the metal that looks like pewter. The mirror is glued into the recess on the front of the frame once the metal is in place. As an alternative, fine-gauge copper or brass foil could also be used to cover the frame.

Metal Mirror

Materials & Equipment

- Tracing paper and pencil
- Thin card (cardboard)
- 18mm (⅝in) MDF (medium-density fibreboard)
- Protective face mask
- Clamp • Jigsaw or hand saw
- Ruler • Scrap wood • Hand drill
- 15mm (½in) flat and 4mm (⅛in) countersink drill bits
- 70cm (28in) batten, 18 x 6mm (⅝ x ¼in)
- Mitre box and hand saw
- Waterproof wood adhesive
- Veneer pins (tacks) • Tack hammer
  Surface filler • Paintbrush
- Water-based acrylic wood primer
- Mid-grey matt emulsion (latex) paint
- Scissors • 36 gauge aluminium foil
- Work gloves • Newspaper
- 125g (4oz) ball-head hammer
- Contact adhesive
- 4mm (⅛in) mirror with polished edges, to fit the recess
- Wood screws • Screwdriver

I Trace the mirror frame and shelf from the templates at the back of the book and enlarge to the desired size. Trace and transfer the photocopies to thin card (cardboard) to make templates. Draw around the templates onto MDF. Wearing a face mask, clamp the MDF and cut out the mirror frame and shelf using a jigsaw or hand saw.

2 Using a pencil and ruler, measure and mark the position of the toothbrush holes on the left-hand side of the shelf. Place the shelf on scrap wood and clamp firmly. Wearing the face mask and using a 15mm (½in) flat drill bit, drill two holes through the shelf where marked. Drill two holes through the base of the mirror frame, 5cm (2in) up from the lower edge. Drill matching pilot holes into the back edge of the shelf.

3 Cut two strips of batten 17.5cm (7in) long and two 15cm (6in) long. Using a mitre box and hand saw, cut all the corners to 45 degrees. Using waterproof wood adhesive, glue and pin the batten centrally to the front of the frame to make a recess for the mirror. Fill the corner joints if necessary.

4 Prime the frame and shelf with one coat of wood primer. Apply two coats of mid-grey emulsion (latex) paint to the frame and shelf and leave to dry.

5 Using scissors, cut a rectangle of aluminium foil to the same dimensions as the outside of the recess, plus 2cm (¾in) all round. Mark the exact size of the recess on the foil. Draw a second rectangle inside this, measuring 1.5cm (½in) smaller all round. Wearing work gloves, cut out the smaller rectangle from the centre of the foil.

6 Cut away a square of foil from the outer corners of the rectangle and snip the inner corners diagonally so that the foil will fold neatly over the recess.

7 Cut rectangles of aluminium foil to cover the sides and lower half of the frame. Cut them slightly larger, so that they can be folded over the sides. Use the template to cut foil for the top of the frame. Place all the foil, including the piece for the recess, on a folded newspaper and tap the back gently with a ball-head hammer.

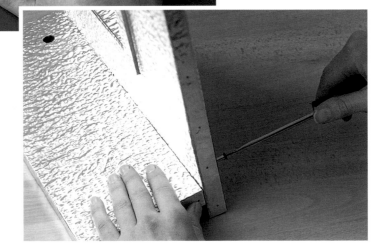

8 Position the foil over the recess. Wearing work gloves, mould it over the batten, pressing it into the corners to fit. Carefully remove the foil. Working in a well-ventilated area, spread contact adhesive on the back of the foil and press into place.

9 Glue the remaining foil to the frame, dimpled side up. Fold the excess foil around the sides, snipping the corners diagonally to fit. Cut a piece of foil to cover the shelf, plus the front and side edges. Mark the position of the toothbrush holes on the foil and cut them out. Hammer the foil as before, then glue it to the shelf, folding the excess over the front and sides.

10 Cut strips of foil 17mm (⅝in) wide. Glue them carefully around the sides of the mirror frame and shelf to neaten them, then pin them in place with veneer pins. Glue the mirror into the recess using contact adhesive. Attach two mirror plates to the sides of the frame. Screw the shelf firmly to the front of the frame.

Women's Head-dresses

In some regions of Tibet, women wear very elaborate head-dresses called *bazhu*. These are large, curved structures decorated with coral and turquoise stones. The women divide their hair into many plaits, which are suspended at either side of the head-dress. Other traditional hairdressing styles include adding coral, turquoise and silver beads to create a stunning curtain of precious stones around the face. In some regions, particularly Kham in the east, women also braid red silk into their hair.

This bead curtain is made from glass, metal and wooden beads strung onto embroidery silk in random patterns to create bands of colour. A star anise is sewn to the end of each string of beads. These seedheads have a lovely warm colour that blends well with the wooden beads.

Beaded Window Screen

Materials & Equipment

- Dark brown embroidery silk
- Scissors
- Fine fuse wire
- Wire cutters
- Silver metal, wood and turquoise glass beads
- Brown cotton sewing thread
- Star anise
- Needle
- Black bamboo cane

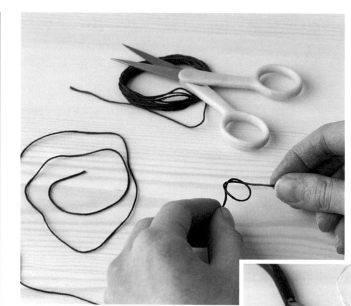

1 Cut lengths of embroidery silk to the height of your window, plus 20cm (8in). Tie a double knot in one end of each piece.

2 Cut a 10cm (4in) length of fuse wire and double it over. Rest the unknotted end of the silk in the bend of the wire and twist the free ends tightly together to make a fine needle.

3 Thread on a short length of silver metal beads. Make sure they can't fall off the end of the silk and re-tie the double knot if necessary, to anchor them firmly.

4 Thread on sections of wood, turquoise and silver beads to make an interesting pattern. Don't worry if you make a mistake: simply remove the beads and re-thread them in a different order until you are happy with the design.

5 Leave about 15cm (6in) of silk above your last bead. Tie a loose loop in the top of the silk. Repeat to make the rest of the bead strings, varying the patterns so that no two are the same.

6 Tie a length of brown cotton thread around the bottom of the string of beads. Hold a star anise against the string and wrap the thread around it several times to bind it in place.

7 Thread the end of the cotton onto a needle and stitch it into the embroidery silk at the back of the star anise to finish it off neatly. Cut a length of black bamboo to fit the window recess and suspend the strings of beads from it.

Tibetan Buildings

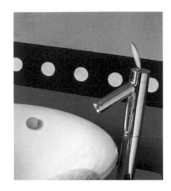

The predominant paint colours on the outsides of Tibetan buildings are earthy and organic. White, yellow ochre, terracotta-red and brown feature prominently, interspersed with flashes of brilliant turquoise-blue and cool green. Traditionally, secular buildings are square-set and made in two or three storeys. The stone walls are laid over wooden poles, which protrude on the outside, giving the walls their characteristic 'spotted' appearance.

The stencilled wall frieze runs around the centre of the room in contrast to the rich red and yellow-ochre walls. The pale cream dots create a strong visual point, drawing in the eye. The colour scheme used is rich and dark and looks wonderful in a large room. Light, creamy terracottas and yellows would be more suitable in a small room.

Stencilled Wall Frieze

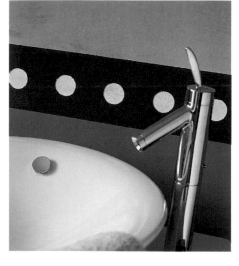

Materials & Equipment

- Oiled manilla stencil card (cardboard)
- Scissors
- Pencil and ruler
- Bottle top, about 3cm (2¼in) in diameter
- Craft knife and cutting mat
- Long metal ruler
- Low-tack masking tape
- Dark brown matt emulsion (latex) paint
- Paintbrush
- Cream matt emulsion (latex) paint
- Old saucer
- Natural sponge

1 Cut a piece of stencil card (cardboard) to the same width as you want your border. Find the middle of the card, then make a mark every 10cm (4in), from the centre out, to determine the middle of each circle. The last mark at either end should be 5cm (2in) from the edge, so trim the card if necessary. Position the bottle top over each mark in turn and draw around it.

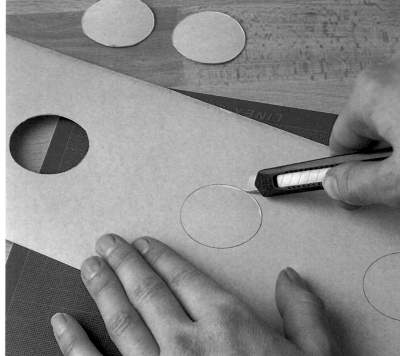

2 Place the stencil card on a cutting mat and cut out each circle using a craft knife. Cut carefully, to make the circles as regular as possible.

3 Using a pencil and long metal ruler, lightly mark out the border on the wall. The border should match the width of the stencil, to make positioning easy.

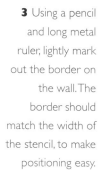

4 Attach strips of low-tack masking tape to the wall just above and below the width of the border. Align the tape carefully with the pencil lines and press it down firmly so that the paint cannot seep underneath.

5 Paint the border with two coats of dark brown emulsion (latex) paint. When the paint is dry, carefully peel off the masking tape.

6 Place the stencil at the start of the border and draw a faint pencil line on the wall at the right-hand edge. Move the stencil along, placing the left-hand side against the pencil line and mark the position of the far end on the wall as before. Continue marking along the border, to make a spacing guide. Attach the stencil to the border with low-tack masking tape.

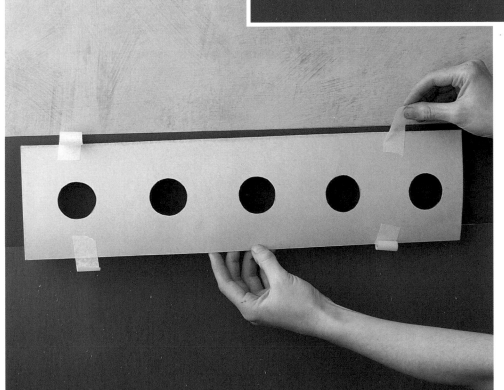

7 Put a small amount of undiluted cream emulsion (latex) paint on an old saucer. Pick up a little paint on the end of a natural sponge and, pressing the card flat against the wall, lightly dab paint over the circles. Untape the stencil and move it along the border to complete the design.

tibet
The
Garden

❝ *Parties and picnics…*

were held together in beautiful and

well-kept gardens that contained

a large variety of flowers and

plants, together with peacocks and

other forms of wildlife. ❞

The World of the Dalai Lama
Gill Farrer-Halls

Mighty Lakes

Tibet, often called the 'Roof of the World', is the highest country on earth, with some areas over 5,000m (16,500ft) above sea level. Some parts, such as the high northern plains, are barren and usually covered in snow all year round, while the southern valleys are fertile, crop-producing areas. Tibet has several thousand lakes, some of which are sacred, and the Tibetan plateau is the source of mighty Asian rivers, such as the Ganges, Mekong and Irrawaddy.

This plain and simple pebble fountain draws its inspiration from the rocky mountain passes and rugged landscape of the isolated plains of Tibet. Gentle streams of water trickle over the smooth, dark pebbles, creating a soothing and contemplative table-top fountain. Silver-painted pebbles, arranged randomly on top, sparkle as they catch the light of the sun.

Table-top Pebble Fountain

Materials & Equipment

- Smooth black pebbles
- Water-based acrylic primer
- Paintbrush
- Silver oil-based enamel craft paint
- Flat artist's paintbrush
- Large, shatterproof plastic bowl
- Varnished wooden tray
- Small fountain pump
- Measuring jug

SAFETY NOTE: Clean the pump regularly, and always operate it according to the manufacturer's instructions.

1 Select about ten small, well-shaped pebbles. Brush off any loose dust, then apply a coat of acrylic primer to each one and leave to dry.

2 Paint the primed pebbles silver. You may have to apply two coats of paint to get an even covering. Leave to dry overnight.

3 Place the bowl centrally on the wooden tray. It is best to construct the fountain where you want it, within easy reach of a power point, as it will be very heavy to move once it is full of pebbles.

4 Place the pump in the centre of the bowl. Adjust the flex so that it sits comfortably against the back of the bowl. Following the pump manufacturer's instructions, fill the bowl with black pebbles.

5 Position the silver pebbles on top of the black, angling them so they catch the light and sparkle.

6 Adjust the bowl until it is in the centre of the tray, with equal amounts of space all round. Arrange larger pebbles around the base of the bowl, filling the space to the edge of the tray.

7 Following the manufacturer's instructions, add the recommended volume of water to the bowl. Switch on the pump, adjusting the height of the water jet as required.

Mani Stones

Piles of inscribed stones can be seen near holy sites, such as along pilgrim passes in Tibet. These are *mani* stones, carved with symbols and prayers, most often *om mani padme hum*, mantra of Bodhisattva Avalokiteshvara, patron deity of Tibet, whence they get their name. The border between Nepal and Tibet, marked by the mountain pass of Langtan, is protected by *mani* stones bearing this auspicious mantra.

These garden slates are painted with natural motifs such as insects and leaves. They are ordinary reclaimed roof slates that have weathered considerably over the years. The motifs are traced down and outlined in off-white acrylic paint, then thin paint is washed over and blotted off to fill in the shapes. The surface of each slate is sealed so that the stones can be left outside and used to line garden borders or walls.

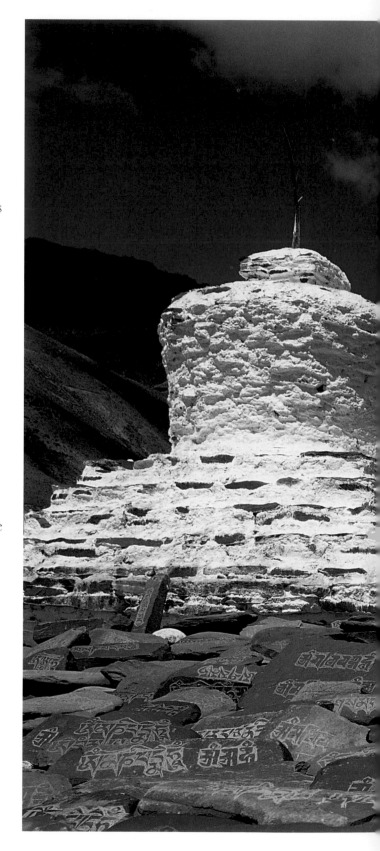

Painted Garden Slates

Materials & Equipment

- Recycled roofing slates
- Tracing paper and pencil
- Transfer paper
- Masking tape
- Cream acrylic paint
- Old saucer
- Thin, pointed, artist's paintbrush
- Flat artist's paintbrush
- Sponge or kitchen roll
- Clear matt acrylic varnish
- Varnishing brush

1 Wash and thoroughly dry the slate. Tape a piece of transfer paper face down onto the front of the slate.

2 Trace the butterfly images from the back of the book. Tape them face down, one above the other, over the transfer paper. Re-draw firmly over the lines to transfer the butterflies to the slate. Remove the paper.

3 Mix cream acrylic paint with a little water on an old saucer. Using a thin, pointed paintbrush, outline the butterflies in paint and leave to dry.

4 Dilute the acrylic paint to a thin wash. Don't make it too watery – it should still cover up the slate when it is applied. Fill in the butterflies, taking care to keep inside the outline.

5 While the paint is still damp, soak up the excess using a sponge or kitchen towel. Remove just enough paint to leave a milky film on the slate.

6 When the paint wash is dry, redefine the butterflies using thicker cream paint and a thin paintbrush. Don't thicken the lines, just strengthen the colour.

7 Once the paint is completely dry, seal the front of the slate with two coats of clear matt varnish. Place in the garden at the back of a border as a decoration.

Nomad Weavers

Traditionally, Tibetan nomads weave cloth by hand, using yarn spun from sheep wool mixed with yak and goat hair. Output includes blankets, sleeping mats and finely woven cloth, called *nambu*, that is used for clothes. The warp threads are threaded onto a horizontal loom, suspended on thick wood supports. The warp is raised and lowered by means of smooth, flat lengths of wood and the weft thread is woven in and out on a shuttle.

The seagrass-bound bamboo candle holders are inspired by the wood and yarn structure of the nomads' looms. Wide bamboo canes are cut to length and stained a dark colour. The base of each cane is tightly wrapped with seagrass twine. The interiors of the candle holders are lined with aluminium foil and the rims are edged with a scalloped foil trim.

Bamboo Candle Holders

SAFETY NOTE: Do not burn the candles too close to shrubs and other plants, and do not leave them to burn unattended. Remove the candles before they burn down to the bamboo.

1 Clamp and cut 50cm (20in) lengths of bamboo. There is a small disc of wood inside the bamboo at each joint, so cut the canes at least 3cm (1¼in) above a joint to make a natural holder for the candle.

Materials & Equipment

- Clamp
- Bamboo canes, 5cm (2in) in diameter
- Ruler and pencil
- Hacksaw
- Protective face mask
- Fine-grade sandpaper
- Water-based medium oak wood stain
- Paintbrush
- Seagrass
- Masking tape
- Scissors
- 36 gauge aluminium foil
- All-purpose adhesive
- Small coin
- Embroidery scissors
- Pillar candles

2 Wearing a face mask, sand the cut edges at either end of the bamboo. Lightly sand the outside of the canes too, so that the wood stain will be absorbed.

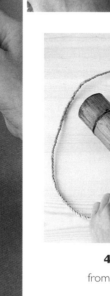

3 Apply a coat of wood stain to the bamboo and leave to dry. If the wood is too pale, apply more coats until the desired shade is obtained.

4 Starting about 20cm (8in) down from the top of a cane, tie on a length of seagrass. Tape the loose end vertically to the side of the bamboo, so that you can cover it neatly.

5 Wrap the seagrass around and around the bamboo, making sure that the coils are straight and closely spaced. Continue wrapping to about 20cm (8in) from the end of the cane, then tie off the seagrass tightly, securing the free end under the last few coils.

6 Cut a strip of aluminium foil to the same depth as the recess at the top of the cane. Curl the foil into a tube, then glue it inside the recess.

7 Cut a circle of foil the same size as the base of the recess. Glue it inside the bamboo, pressing it flat against the bottom of the recess.

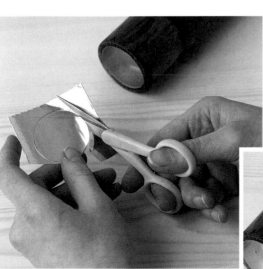

8 Cut a strip of foil 12mm (½in) wide. Place a small coin on the foil, overlapping the edge, then draw around it to make a scalloped pattern along the foil strip.

9 Cut out the edge of the strip using embroidery scissors. Glue the foil around the top of the cane. Plant the cane securely in the ground, about 20cm (8in) deep (as far as the start of the seagrass) and insert a snugly fitting pillar candle.

Templates

All templates shown actual size unless otherwise stated.

Flower Table Runner   p18

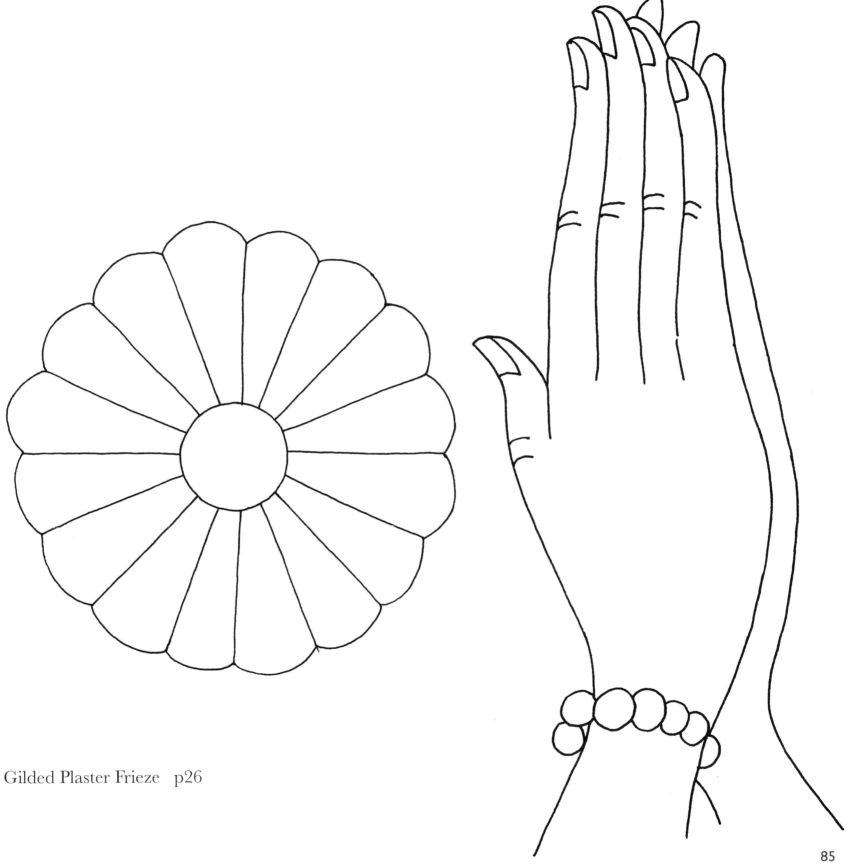

Gilded Plaster Frieze   p26

Banded Floor Cloth p32

Enlarge by 200%

Banded Floor Cloth   p32

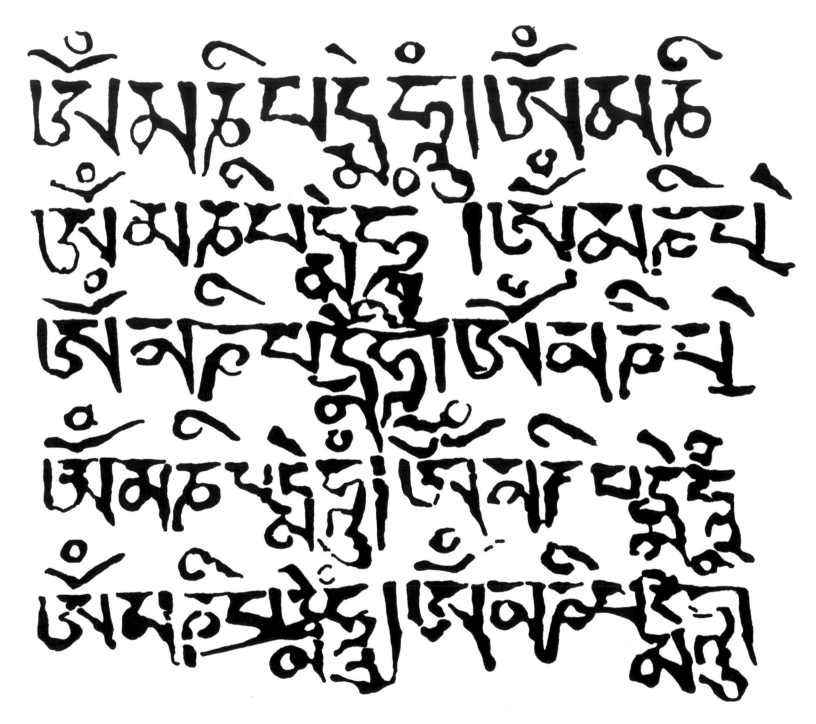

Pocket Window Blind   p50

Use at size required

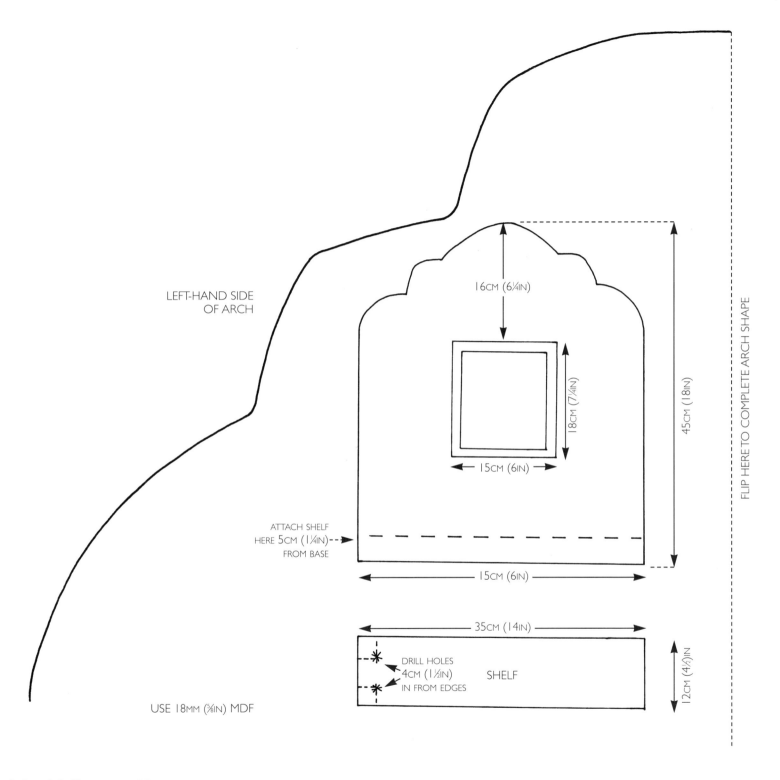

LEFT-HAND SIDE
OF ARCH

16CM (6¼IN)

18CM (7¼IN)

15CM (6IN)

45CM (18IN)

FLIP HERE TO COMPLETE ARCH SHAPE

ATTACH SHELF
HERE 5CM (1¼IN)
FROM BASE

15CM (6IN)

35CM (14IN)

12CM (4½)IN

DRILL HOLES
4CM (1½IN)
IN FROM EDGES

SHELF

USE 18MM (⅝IN) MDF

Metal Mirror p60

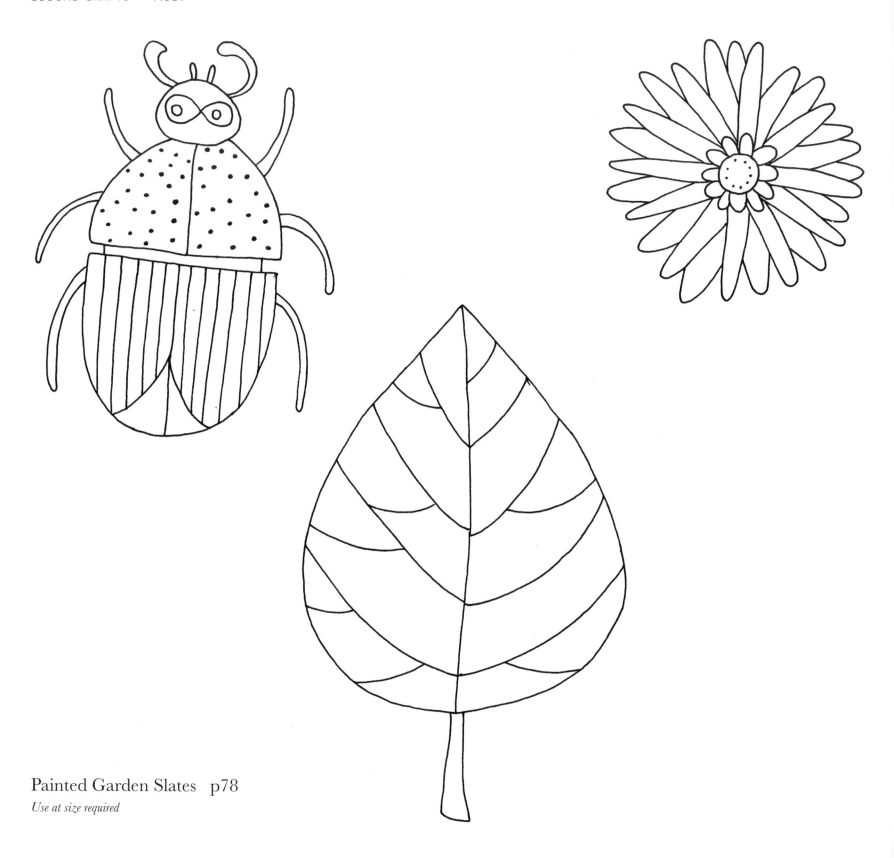

Painted Garden Slates   p78

Use at size required

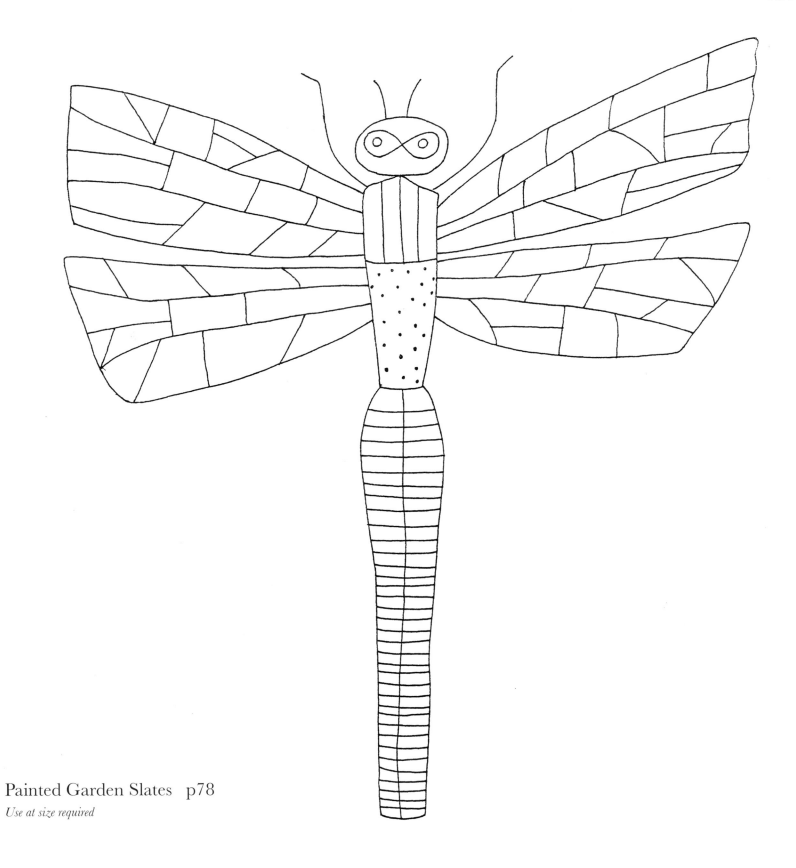

Painted Garden Slates p78

Use at size required

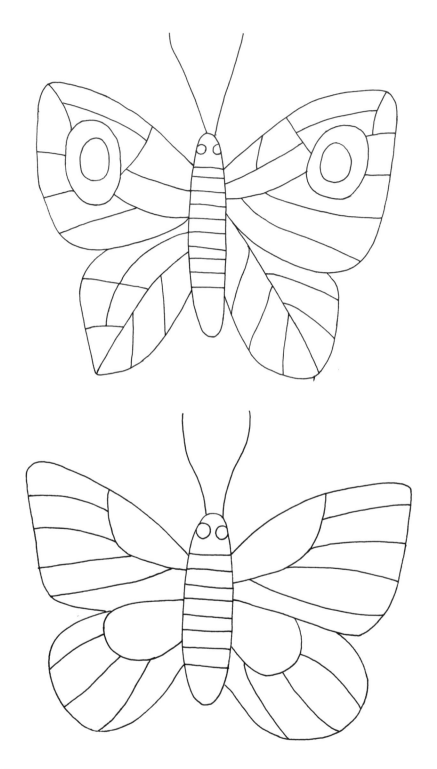

Painted Garden Slates   p78

Use at size required

Painted Garden Slates   p78

Use at size required

Further Information

Cultural Organizations

Meridian Trust
A charitable organization dedicated to the
preservation of Tibetan culture and Buddhism
through film and video.
website: www.meridian-trust.org
e-mail: info@meridian-trust.org

Tibet Foundation
2 Bloomsbury Way
London WC1
Tel: 020 7404 2889

Tibet House
22 West 15th Street
New York, NY 10011
Tel: (212) 807-0563
Fax: (212) 807-0565
website: www.tibethouse.org

Tibet Society
114 Tottenham Court Road
London W1
Tel: 020 7383 7533
website: www.tibet-society.org.uk

UK Suppliers

J W Bollom
314 Old Brompton Street
London SW5
Tel: 020 7370 3252
Felt

The Cane Store
Blackstock Road
London N4
Tel: 020 7354 4210
Bamboo

Ells and Farrier
20 Beak Street
London W1
Tel: 020 7629 9964
Beads

McCulloch and Wallis Ltd
25 Dering Street
London W1
Tel: 020 7629 0311
Trimmings

VV Rouleaux Ltd
6 Marylebone High Street
London W1
Tel: 020 7224 5179
Trimmings

Alec Tiranti
27 Warren St.
London W1
Tel: 0207 636 8565
Aluminium foil

US Suppliers

Blanks Fabric
6709 Whitestone Road
Baltimore, MD 21207
Tel: (410) 944-0040
Fax: (410) 298-2834
website: www.blanksfab.com
Felt and other speciality fabrics

Frank's Cane and Rush Supply
7252 Heil Avenue
Huntington Beach, CA 92647
Tel: (714) 847-0707
Fax: (714) 843-5645
website: www.franksupply.com
Bamboo

Pearl Paint
308 Canal Street
New York, NY 10013
(additional stores throughout the US)
Tel: (800) 221-6845 (ext. 2297)
website: www.pearlpaint.com
Dutch metal leaf and other art supplies

WFR Ribbon Inc.
259 Center Street
Phillipsburg, NJ 08865
Tel: (908) 454-7700
Fax: (908) 454-0657
For a list of retailers of Mokuba ribbons,
please send a self-addressed envelope to
Customer Service at the above address.

Potala Corporation
9 East 36th Street
New York, NY 10016
Tel: (212) 251-0360
Fax: (212) 696-0431
website: www.potala.com
Retailer and wholesaler of Tibetan carpets,
handicrafts, clothing, books and incense.
Owned by the Tibetan Government in Exile.

Index

Page numbers in *italics* indicate illustrations; page numbers in **bold** indicate templates and diagrams.

Acknowledgements

Author's Acknowledgements

I would like to thank all the people who made producing this book such a pleasure: Neil Hadfield, as ever, for his support and enthusiasm, and for making the Beaten Metal Mirror; Ali Myer and Cheryl Brown for their vision and hard work, especially at the start of the project; Stewart Grant for his great photography and, with Ginette Chapman, his hospitality; Ian Cumming at Tibet Images for supplying such wonderful inspirational pictures; Lisa Brown for her sensitive styling; Carmen for cheerfully working late; Sarah Widdicombe for her sharp eyes and Lindsay Porter, who, with Ali Myer, pulled it all together with such style.

Publishers' Acknowledgements

The publishers would like to thank the following for lending items for photography:

The Kitchen
Phoenix chairs: Purves and Purves (0870 603 0205); bowls: Neal Street East (020 7240 0135); napkins: The Pier (020 7814 5004); napkin rings: Nice Irmas (020 8343 9766)

The Living Room
Sofa, table: The Pier (020 7814 5004); shoes, bag, bowl, tassels, red cushion, floor cushion: Neal Street East (020 7240 0135); blue cushion: Nice Irmas (020 8343 9766)

The Bedroom
Bed, tea set: Muji (020 7323 2208); table: Nice Irmas (020 8343 9766); cushions: Next Home (08702 435 435); boxed unit, candle shades, rug: The Pier (020 7814 5004); shoes, vase, Saki set, tray: Neal Street East (020 7240 0135)

The Bathroom
Philippe Starck sink: CP Hart (020 7902 1000); towels: Christy (0345 585252); baskets with lids, rattan laundry basket: Next Home (08702 435 435); basket with handles, soap, bag: Neal Street East (020 7240 0135)

The Garden
Chair: Purves and Purves (0870 603 0205)

Picture Credits

All photographs are by Stewart Grant, except the following: Tibet Images/Diane Barker pages 58–9, 80–1; Tibet Images/Stephen Batchelor pages 20–1; Tibet Images/Ian Cumming pages 24–5, 30–1, 38–9, 48–9, 66–7, 76–7; Tibet Images/Yeo Dong-Wan pages 72–3; Tibet Images/Barry Green pages 52-3; Tibet Images/Norma Joseph pages 16–17, 34–5; Tibet Images/Catherine Platt pages 44–5; Tibet Images/Stone Routes pages 62–3.

Front cover, below: Tibet Images/Ian Cumming

The Mantra template, page 88, is reproduced from *Tibetan Buddhism*, L Austin Waddell, Dover Books, 1972

Bibliography

Touching Tibet, Niema Ash, TravellersEye Ltd, 1999

An Illustrated Encyclopaedia of Traditional Symbols, J C Cooper, Thames and Hudson, 1990

Weaving in Nepal, Susi Dunsmore, Overseas Development National Resources Institute, 1990

The World of the Dalai Lama, Gill Farrer-Halls, Thorsons, 1998

Art of Tibet, Robert E Fisher, Thames and Hudson, 1997

Tibetan Voices – A Traditional Memoir, Brian Harris, Pomegranate Artbooks, 1996

World Crafts, Jacqueline Herald, Charles Letts, 1992

The Wonders of Tibet, Chen Heyi, China Pictorial Publishing House, 1994

Tibet, Mayhew, Bellezza, Wheeler and Taylor, Lonely Planet Publications, 1999

Tibetan Buddhism, L Austin Waddell, Dover Books, 1972

Tibet, Michael Willis, Duncan Baird Publishers, 1999

For further information about the author, visit her website at www.marionelliot.co.uk